WHEN I GROW UP

I WANT TO BE A LIST OF

FURTHER POSSIBILITIES

Chen Chen was born in 1989 in Xiamen, China, and "grew up" in Massachusetts in the US. His first book-length collection, *When I Grow Up I Want to Be a List of Further Possibilities* (BOA Editions, US, 2017; Bloodaxe Books, UK, 2019), was longlisted for the National Book Award and won the A. Poulin, Jr. Poetry Prize, the Great Lakes Colleges Association (GLCA) New Writers Award, the Texas Book Award for Poetry, and the Thom Gunn Award for Gay Poetry. The book was also a finalist for the Lambda Literary Award for Gay Poetry and named a Stonewall Honor Book. His second collection, *Your Emergency Contact Has Experienced an Emergency*, is published by Bloodaxe Books in the UK and BOA Editions in the US in 2022.

He is also the author of a collection of essays, *In Cahoots with the Rabbit God* (Noemi Press, 2023), and four chapbooks, most recently *GESUNDHEIT!* (Glass Poetry Press, 2019), a collaboration with Sam Herschel Wein. Chen's work appears in many publications, including *Staying Human* and three editions of *The Best American Poetry*. His poems have been translated into French, Greek, Russian, and Spanish. He has received two Pushcart Prizes and fellowships from Kundiman, the National Endowment for the Arts, and United States Artists. He holds an MFA from Syracuse University and a PhD from Texas Tech University. He was the 2018–2022 Jacob Ziskind Poet-in-Residence at Brandeis University. He serves on the poetry faculty for the low-residency MFA programs at New England College and Stonecoast. He edits the Twitter-based journal *the lickety~split* and with a brilliant team he edits *Underblong*. He lives with his partner, Jeff Gilbert, and their pug, Mr Rupert Giles.

CHEN CHEN

WHEN I GROW UP
I WANT TO BE A LIST OF
FURTHER POSSIBILITIES

FOREWORD BY
JERICHO BROWN

BLOODAXE BOOKS

Copyright © Chen Chen 2017, 2019.
Foreword copyright © Jericho Brown 2017, 2019

ISBN: 978 1 78037 486 4

First published in the USA
by BOA Editions in 2017.

First published in the UK in 2019 by
Bloodaxe Books Ltd,
Eastburn,
South Park,
Hexham,
Northumberland NE46 1BS.

www.bloodaxebooks.com
For further information about Bloodaxe titles
please visit our website and join our mailing list
or write to the above address for a catalogue

Supported using public funding by
ARTS COUNCIL
ENGLAND

Cover design: Neil Astley & Pamela Robertson-Pearce.

Digital reprint of the 2019 Bloodaxe Books edition.

for my family,
my teachers,
& Jeff Gilbert

in loving memory of Ruthann Johnson

Contents

3

◎

The charm, intention, expectancy, and wonder in the title *When I Grow Up I Want to Be a List of Further Possibilities* point directly to the powers particular and talents specific to Chen Chen as a poet. The greatest achievement of this book is its singular and sustained voice, poem after poem of a speaker whose obsessive and curious nature is that of an adult who refuses to give up seeing through the eyes of an adolescent, one who believes that the world is a malleable place and that asking the right questions changes its form.

The major question of this book is how to feel. What is the proper emotional response to parents who physically attack us, to friends and family who object to our work as artists, to a nation that finds subtle ways to deny our citizenship while requiring our taxes? But while those questions are germane to Chen's writing, the answers are what make this collection a unique contribution to all of poetry. Though reasons for the quest are morbid, this is a poet who knows the journey won't begin or end if he does not take every step in humor, the earliest poems in the book preparing us for comic delight with lines like, "I am not the heterosexual neat freak my mother raised me to be" and—in a meditation on the nature of God—"God sent an angel. One of his least qualified, though. Fluent only in / Lemme get back to you. The angel sounded like me, early twenties, / unpaid interning."

In these and other poems, comedy is juxtaposed with a sense of wonder characterized by the surreal as an element of the quotidian. As Chen's speaker meanders discursively toward wisdom, he comes upon images that lead the reader to question what we expect to see when reading poetry with lines such as, "Dreaming of one day being as fearless as a mango" and "I am making my loneliness small. So small it fits on a postcard / a baby rabbit could eat" and

> My dream in the motels that my father's scholarship
> was a type of ship & soon we'd get to ride it
> & reach Massachusetts, a vast
> snowy island.

This last set of lines from the poem "Things Stuck in Other Things Where They Don't Belong" is one of several examples of how every word manages a new kind of weight as each poem and the book itself progress. The uprootedness of "motels" and the transmigration of "ship" and the colonization of "Massachusetts" are a part of the skilled and seemingly childlike play that allows Chen to see the ordinary as the oddity, leading him to language where the introspective experience is made more full by becoming the site for political experiences, as in these lines from "Nature Poem":

> Earlier today, outside the cabin, the sudden deer were a supreme
> headache of beauty. Don't they know I am trying to be alone
> & at peace? In theory I am alone & really I am hidden,
> which is a fine temporary substitute for peace, except I still
>
> have email, which is how I receive my horoscope, & even here
> in the wooded dark I receive yet another email mistaking me
> for another Chen. I add this to a folder, which also includes
> emails sent to my address but addressed to Chang,
>
> Chin, Cheung. Once, in a Starbucks, the cashier
> was convinced I was Chad. Once, in a Starbucks, the cashier
> did not quite finish the n on my Chen, & when my tall mocha was ready,
> they called out for Cher. I preferred this by far, but began to think
>
> the problem was Starbucks. Why can't you see me? Why can't I stop
> needing you to see me? For someone who looks like you
> to look at me, even as the coffee accident
> is happening to my second favorite shirt?

This is an astounding meeting of peace with empire, of nature with technology, and of the individual with the perception others have that he couldn't possibly be individual at all. And all of this happens in the midst of being mistaken for Cher and an attention to what magic language can make: "the sudden deer were a supreme / headache of beauty." The poem ends in questions where, again, the speaker is most hungry to know how to be, how to feel. And of course, he won't be satisfied with any answer until he has thoroughly reviewed every possibility, every option for becoming a more whole self in the most intimate of moments, as in "Second Thoughts on a Winter Afternoon":

> Your mother is sick & all I can think of is how sick's
> also a word for "cool," like "ill," though maybe "ill"
>
> is becoming outdated, & "sick" too, & actually it's a lie
> I can only think of that, I can also think of my mother,
>
> how your mother's pancreatic cancer doesn't sound
> as pretty as the problem my mother has with her heart,

heartbeat, & I can even think my mother has it tougher,
though it isn't cancer, & of course I'd think that, she's mom,

mommy, though of course this woman is mom, mommy
to you, & mommy is very sick . . .

When I Grow Up I Want to Be a List of Further Possibilities is a collection that manages the meditative as well as it wields the rant, and it often achieves both of these in a single poem. This is necessary in a book where God so often gets beseeched, denied, and honored. For Chen Chen, poetry is the place where the sacred is reached through the profane, or as he writes in "Talking to God About Heaven from the Bed of a Heathen":

I know, though, that there are believers who don't believe
out of fear solely. They actually love you. They reach out

& receive your touch. Like a friend, like a boyfriend, like the boy
beside me, overheating, reeking of sweat . . .

It is no wonder that this book is a library of allusions to forbears including Paul Celan, Allen Ginsberg, Franz Kafka, Pablo Neruda, Christopher Smart, and Georg Trakl. The formal inventiveness of these poems reflects a mind unsatisfied with easy answers, a poet preoccupied with new ways to ask questions, a very young and ambitious voice who, in the poem "Spell to Find Family," proclaims:

My job is to trick adults

into knowing they have
hearts.

. . . My job is to trick

myself into believing
there are new ways
to find impossible honey.

This is a stunning debut and the first of what is bound to be several beautifully necessary books.

Jericho Brown
Atlanta

WHEN I GROW UP

I WANT TO BE

A LIST OF

FURTHER POSSIBILITIES

SELF-PORTRAIT AS SO MUCH POTENTIAL

Dreaming of one day being as fearless as a mango.

As friendly as a tomato. Merciless to chin & shirtfront.

Realizing I hate the word "sip."

But that's all I do.

I drink. So slowly.

& say I'm tasting it. When I'm just bad at taking in liquid.

I'm no mango or tomato. I'm a rusty yawn in a rumored year. I'm an arctic attic.

Come amble & ampersand in the slippery polar clutter.

I am not the heterosexual neat freak my mother raised me to be.

I am a gay sipper, & my mother has placed what's left of her hope on my brothers.

She wants them to gulp up the world, spit out solid degrees, responsible
    grandchildren ready to gobble.

They will be better than mangoes, my brothers.

Though I have trouble imagining what that could be.

Flying mangoes, perhaps. Flying mango-tomato hybrids. Beautiful sons.

1

God sent an angel. One of his least qualified, though. Fluent only in
Lemme get back to you. The angel sounded like me, early twenties,
unpaid interning. Proficient in fetching coffee, sending super
vague emails. It got so bad God personally had to speak to me.
This was annoying because I'm not a religious person. I thought
I'd made this clear to God by reading Harry Potter & not attending
church except for gay weddings. God did not listen to me. God is
not a good listener. I said Stop it please, I'll give you wedding cake,
money, candy, marijuana. Go talk to married people, politicians,
children, reality TV stars. I'll even set up a booth for you,
then everyone who wants to talk to you can do so
without the stuffy house of worship, the stuffier middlemen,
& the football blimps that accidentally intercept prayers
on their way to heaven. I'll keep the booth decorations simple
but attractive: stickers of angels & cats, because I'm not religious
but didn't people worship cats? Thing is, God couldn't take a hint.
My doctor said to eat an apple every day. My best friend said to stop
sleeping with guys with messiah complexes. My mother said she is
pretty sure she had sex with my father so I can't be some new
Asian Jesus. I tried to enrage God by saying things like When I asked
my mother about you, she was in the middle of making dinner
so she just said Too busy. I tried to confuse God by saying I am
a made-up dinosaur & a real dinosaur & who knows maybe
I love you, but then God ended up relating to me. God said I am
a good dinosaur but also sort of evil & sometimes loving no one.
It rained & we stayed inside. Played a few rounds of backgammon.
We used our indoor voices. It got so quiet I asked God
about the afterlife. Its existence, human continued existence.
He said Oh. That. Then sent his angel again. Who said Ummmmmmm.
I never heard from God or his rookie angel after that. I miss them.
Like creatures I made up or found in a book, then got to know a bit.

In the Hospital

My mother was in the hospital & everyone wanted to be my friend.
But I was busy making a list: good dog, bad citizen, short
skeleton, tall mocha. Typical Tuesday.
My mother was in the hospital & no one wanted to be her friend.
Everyone wanted to be soft cooing sympathies. Very reasonable
pigeons. No one had the time & our solution to it
was to buy shinier watches. We were enamored with
what our wrists could declare. My mother was in the hospital
& I didn't want to be her friend. Typical son. Tall latte, short tale,
bad plot, great wifi in the atypical café. My mother was in the hospital
& she didn't want to be her friend. She wanted to be the family
grocery list. Low-fat yogurt, firm tofu. She didn't trust my father
to be it. *You always forget something,* she said, *even when
I do the list for you. Even then.*

Summer Was Forever

Time dripped from the faucet like a magician's botched trick.
I did not want to applaud it. I stood to one side & thought,
What it's time for is a garden. Or a croissant factory. What kind
of work do I need to be doing? My parents said: *Doctor,*
married to lawyer. The faucet said: *Drip, drop,*
your life sucks. But sometimes no one said anything & I saw
him, the local paper boy on his route. His beanstalk frame
& fragile bicycle. & I knew: we would be so terribly
happy. Our work would be simple. Our kissing would rhyme
with cardiac arrest. Birds would overthrow the cathedral towers.
I would have a magician's hair, full of sleeves & saws,
unashamed to tell the whole town our first date was
in a leaky faucet factory. How we fell in love during jumps
on his tragic uncle's trampoline. We fell in love in midair.

Race to the Tree

1.

I was 13 & it was night & without
even knowing it, I had successfully
evaded the Amherst police
for 4, 5 hours. It was night & without
    having committed any crimes,
    I was pursued, looked into
    by the Amherst police.
    Well, perhaps I'd trespassed:

scrambled up a tree past mine
& its bedtime. Stoic & oak,
it once served with dignity
as "safety." It stood, so close
    to my family's apartment
    it was pathetic the police
    couldn't find me, so close
    the oak seemed to be

ours. But it wasn't—every oak
& pine & birch in the complex belonged
to the landlord, whether or not
he'd climbed each one himself.
    I had scaled this old "safe" tree
    with my running shoes, planning
    to run away—if not far away enough,
    then for long away enough

that my parents would start to miss me.
I was 13 & it was night & all night I stared
at the moon from my tree, willing myself to think
not of *them*, but of how it would taste
    to kiss, to be kissed, oh
    moon, for a long time, for the first time,

to be k-i-s-s-i-n-g in this
or any tree . . .

2.

I wanted to kiss a boy
on the throat, not the soft, smooth
neck but the protruding, tough
core of a boy's throat, the part
        named after the very first boy
        & the stupid fruit his girlfriend
        made him eat. His girlfriend's
        ugly, I thought in my tree, I'd be

much better for him. By dawn I was
still 13 & kissless, but had made it
(using my spy & JV track skills)
8 blocks away, without being detected,
        to the University, the glass
        & concrete country where my parents
        put on their best American accents
        & smiles, to earn degrees

the equivalents of which they'd already
earned in China. I was 13 & wouldn't have
said it so succinctly, but I knew something
about the sadness of the facts, oh
        moon, hungry moon, unkissed
        & silent, I would kiss you.
        In that moment though, I decided
        to spit & kick

at the gray concrete, recalling Mom & Dad's
idiot faces, yelling at me. I was 13
& it was morning & the concrete
deserved my punishment & my
        climbing it like a tree & my

installing myself as The Landlord
here & everywhere & everyone
should see. It was morning

& my eyes hurt in the growing
light. & then, as the sun poured its useless
gold on all the solid gray, as I was about to
reach the top
  of the slanted edge of a wall,
  for the first time my speedy
  stealthy sneakers failed me—
  & I slipped.

3.

Ankle-twisted & whimpering, I limped
back home. My mother rushed out
& greeted me with pale-faced
silence, then a command to get
  in the car. As she drove me back
  to campus, this time to the student
  clinic, she told me that she had called
  & called the police, who had told her

it'll be alright, we'll find him, though they couldn't,
hadn't, maybe didn't even bother to try.
I watched my mother's fingers
on the steering wheel.
  An hour later, I boarded the bus to school
  on crutches. At school I told the boy
  I liked, the boy with the best
  mile times on the team,

that I was just getting some extra practice
& wasn't careful & guess now I'll never be as good
as you this season. He looked at me
for a moment. Looked away.

I didn't tell him I spent all night in a tree
because my mother slapped me
after I told her I might be gay.
I didn't tell him that I hit her back,

that my father tried holding us apart
like the universe's saddest referee.
I didn't show the boy the bruise
I didn't show the doctor.
     I said, *Good luck at the race today*,
     then closed my eyes, thought of night,
     of the moon bobbing through it,
     like an Adam's apple

plucked out, bobbing through a dark
absence of throat, oh
silent & unkissed—that's how I wanted
you to suffer, too, boy who wouldn't
     look at me. Seeing you run so beautifully
     on the track that afternoon, I wanted you
     to suffocate, breath-starved from all the miles
     you'd run away from me.

The sun sets like a whispered regret behind the hills or is that a mountain.
Moths come to the screen door as if that was what they were made for.
Moth for screen door. & vice versa.
I don't have time for their secrets tonight.
I am making my loneliness small. So small it fits on a postcard
a baby rabbit could eat.
The sun sets like an expensive fragrance. Like the memory of a neck.
The coyotes come but don't they know I've named that rabbit, stay away.
Stay far.
The sun sets like a new regret like a flute I am learning to play
& I'm bad at it. Progress is slow.
It's like saying *tapioca pudding* into the phone.
& the phone doesn't work, I just want its weight pressed against my ear
until my ear is sticky.
I'm in the mood for facts.
Big globs of them. Big adult rabbits of science.
There's a town in Upstate New York called Esperance where the gravity
works fine.
Esperance, NY as if "hope" in French is a higher quality hope.
Made of jewels & brie.
The sun sets like a science special I hated once.

Self-Portrait With & Without

With dried cranberries. Without a driver's license. With my mother's
mother's worry. Without, till recently, my father's glasses. With an A in English,
a C in chemistry. With my mother saying, *You have to be three times better
than the white kids, at everything.* Without a dog or cat. With a fish.
With a fish I talked to before bed, telling him my ideas for new kinds
of candy. With a tutor in Mandarin. With the 1986 low-budget live-action
TV version of *Journey to the West.* With Monkey King's quest for redemption,
Buddhism through monster-of-the-week battle sequences. With thinking
I've grown up now because I regularly check the news in the morning.
With the morning the children, spared or missed by the child with a gun,
go back to school, make the same jokes they made three Mondays ago
but in a different voice. With the younger brother who is taller
than I am. With the youngest brother who wants to go
to art school. With my mother's multiplying worries. With my brothers,
my brothers. With the cry of bats. With the salt of circumstance.
Without citizenship. With the white boy in ninth grade who called me
ugly. Without my father, for a year, because he had to move away,
to the one job he could find, on the other side of the state. With his money,
transferred to my mother. With William Carlos Williams. With the local
library. With yet another bake sale for Honduras in Massachusetts suburbia.
With the earthquake in my other country. With my mother's long-distance calls.
With my aunt's calls from China, when the towers fell.
How far are you from New York? How far are you from New York?
With cities fueled by scars. With the footprint of a star. With the white boy
I liked. With him calling me ugly. With my knees on the floor. With my hands
begging for straighter teeth, lighter skin, blue eyes, green eyes,
any eyes brighter, other than mine.

First Light

I like to say we left at first light
        with Chairman Mao himself chasing us in a police car,
my father fighting him off with firecrackers,
        even though Mao was already over a decade
dead, & my mother says all my father did
        during the Cultural Revolution was teach math,
which he was not qualified to teach, & swim & sunbathe
        around Piano Island, a place I never read about
in my American textbooks, a place everybody in the family
        says they took me to, & that I loved.
What is it, to remember nothing, of what one loved?
        To have forgotten the faces one first kissed?
They ask if I remember them, the aunts, the uncles,
        & I say *Yes it's coming back,* I say *Of course,*
when it's *No not at all,* because when I last saw them
        I was three, & the China of my first three years
is largely make-believe, my vast invented country,
        my dream before I knew the word "dream,"
my father's martial arts films plus a teaspoon-taste
        of history. I like to say we left at first light,
we had to, my parents had been unmasked as the famous
        kung fu crime-fighting couple of the Southern provinces,
& the Hong Kong mafia was after us. I like to say
        we were helped by a handsome mysterious Northerner,
who turned out himself to be a kung fu master.
        I don't like to say, I don't remember crying.
No embracing in the airport, sobbing. I don't remember
        feeling bad, leaving China.
I like to say we left at first light, we snuck off
        on some secret adventure, while the others were
still sleeping, still blanketed, warm
        in their memories of us.
What do I remember of crying? When my mother slapped me
        for being *dirty, diseased, led astray by Western devils,*

a dirty, bad son, I cried, thirteen, already too old,
　　　　too male for crying. When my father said *Get out,*
never come back, I cried & ran, threw myself into night.
　　　　Then returned, at first light, I don't remember exactly
why, or what exactly came next. One memory claims
　　　　my mother rushed into the pink dawn bright
to see what had happened, reaching toward me with her hands,
　　　　& I wanted to say *No. Don't touch me.*
Another memory insists the front door had simply been left
　　　　unlocked, & I slipped right through, found my room,
my bed, which felt somehow smaller, & fell asleep, for hours,
　　　　before my mother (anybody) seemed to notice.
I'm not certain which is the correct version, but what stays with me
　　　　is the leaving, the cry, the country splintering.
It's been another five years since my mother has seen her sisters,
　　　　her own mother, who recently had a stroke, who has trouble
recalling who, why. *I feel awful,* my mother says,
　　　　not going back at once to see her. But too much is happening here.
Here, she says, as though it's the most difficult,
　　　　least forgivable English word.
What would my mother say, if she were the one writing?
　　　　How would her voice sound? Which is really to ask, what is
my best guess, my invented, translated (Chinese-to-English,
　　　　English-to-English) mother's voice? She might say:
We left at first light, we had to, the flight was early,
　　　　in early spring. *Go,* my mother urged, *what are you doing,*
waving at me, crying? Get on that plane before it leaves without you.
　　　　It was spring & I could smell it, despite the sterile glass
& metal of the airport—scent of my mother's just-washed hair,
　　　　of the just-born flowers of fields we passed on the car ride over,
how I did not know those flowers were already
　　　　memory, how I thought I could smell them, boarding the plane,
the strange tunnel full of their aroma, their names
　　　　I once knew, & my mother's long black hair—so impossible now.
Why did I never consider how different spring could smell, feel,
　　　　elsewhere? First light, last scent, lost
country. First & deepest severance that should have
　　　　prepared me for all others.

HOW I BECAME SAGACIOUS

The day the window grew till it no longer fit the house
      was the night I decided to leave.
I carried in my snake mouth a boxful
      of carnal autobiographies.
I went in search of a face without theory.
      The window went on to sing a throb of deer
melody. The shape, the day of my belly sobbed
      with the outline of a deer.
The clouds were a mouth-shaped poison,
      & ready. I saw violence in anything
with a face. I wished for a place big enough for grief,
      & all I got was more grief, plus *People* magazine.
There were some inside things I was going to make
      outside things, just for one person in a godless
living room, full of passé plants. Now what?
      So blah & bewildered, my hands
have turned out to be no bee,
      all bumble, unable to tell the difference
between the floor & the ground. They feel dirt,
      but it feels like something they made.

ELEGY

My shoes were growing more powerful
with each day. I walked in the country of letters,

its fields of eyes belonging to my lost sister—
dark eyes that early closed, or forgot

to open. I have not been back in some time,
though often I walk to my office, daydreaming

of that country's fashions, the clothes of its citizens
like the clothes of my dearest dead or unborn.

In the heaven of letters, I will not walk.
I will not strip the golden clothes from my lover,

the wheat. I will stand, stay with the trees before me,
their ancient charisma that cares for me.

Like all scholars in any sort of heaven, I will study
the metaphysics of madness. I will find

that the littler the light, the better it tastes.
On Earth lately, I've been looking at everyone

like I love them, & maybe I do. Or maybe I only love
one person, & I'm beaming from it. Or actually

I just love myself, & I want people to know.
It seems the dead are busy with work we cannot

comprehend. & like parents, they don't want to tell you
what their jobs really consist of, how much they make.

They don't want to scare you, the dead. With what's
left of their ankles, with their new secret wishes.

the little strangers   upon entering   the quiet   the Shh   the please
follow the signs   walk   do not run   do not fall down   or in love
be respectful of the others in the space   do not offer them food
or drink   especially French fries   or any tokens of deep affection
Everyone is trying their best   please   remain calm   you may
experience some turbulence   flatulence   a touch of total nauseating
love   that is normal   but keep it   under control   Look   the head
librarian has   turned on the fasten seatbelt sign   please return
to your desk   & duck   & fasten   & calm   & Shh   & do not
& starboard   & roger that   & no fries   & do not
claw the walls   saying you love   PBS
The other passengers are trying their best   to buy tomato soup
to sell their boots   to wear the socks their mothers always
buy for them   Do not disturb them   Do however report any suspicious
weathers   Crouch   to sniff out large unattended   clouds   If you
smell something   say something   say   Nice socks   nice boots
nice tomato soup   & the clouds will vanish   Do not say   LeVar Burton
is my lover   & Mr. Rogers my dearest friend   quick   LeVar   Rogers
let us find what we need   in this great country   of burning

2

SONG WITH A LYRIC FROM ALLEN GINSBERG

The trees, a madness of white & wind,
we, a madness of sweat & rope,
ropes of semen lassoing each other, closer—

our competing, conspiring tongues, nipples,
armpits, the terribly neglected inside bits
of our elbows, which we've dubbed "bowpits,"

& kiss. & my mind sometimes wanders during,
but it's OK, I'm thinking of Ginsberg's letters
to friends & lovers, how once I read a small hill

of them in the library & some were poems & some
were prayers, cries, ejaculate, & now all I remember
is *I love you I love you,* & how long would it take

to read all the world's letters, sent (& unsent),
every *I love you (I love you)*, & can you believe the trees,
out our bedroom window, what a turn-on, nature,

even in winter, no I don't think the earth ever stops
being alive, just ask Allen or his boyfriend Walt
or anyone who's recently had an orgasm or two.

When I fall asleep, in the after-love dream, the old man
at the intersection again, waiting for the light to change—
a cone of black raspberry ice cream in hand & some of it

messing his great white beard as he dips down to lick.
His look, not of joy but impatience, like him & ice cream
got a meeting, got other hims & ice creams to see.

Talented Human Beings

Every day I am asked to care about white people,
especially if they've been kidnapped overseas
or are experiencing marital problems in New England,
on screens large & small. I am told American
lives are in danger, American libidos.

In 2042, when white people become the minority,
will the news continue to chirp *American lives are in danger*
or will we have to specify white & add *no, really*
& *their lives matter, too.* Pop Quiz: Who was
Vincent Chin? Theresa Hak Kyung Cha?

Group Project: Name one book by Maxine Hong Kingston
not titled *The Woman Warrior.* In college I strived
to be an Asian American sex symbol, but got too busy
trying to get a hot white boy to text me back.
One summer, to further the cause, I jerked off

exclusively to Koh Masaki, a Japanese gay porn star.
A big star, with his exquisite scruff, highly
responsive nipples, tireless hips gold & glistening.
But then I felt conflicted, listening to relatives in China
lament the popularity of Japanese cars. But Chinese porn

wasn't as good. Low production values, too much
story. & then Koh Masaki died, at 29, following
complications from an appendix operation. A tragically
un-epic way to go. Not a martyr, writer, "real" actor,
no activist, not even Asian American, just someone

who looked like me, if I worked out more than twice a year,
& could make tonguing the hairy sweat from a man's ass
look like a Hiroshige, & had the marathon heart to fuck
the beautiful out of five not-as-well-paid
but also very talented human beings.

To the Guanacos at the Syracuse Zoo

I'm sorry I would've skipped past your exhibit
on my quest for the elephants, if not
for my boyfriend's shouting, *Look, llamas!*
I'm sorry I then called out *Llamas!* twice,
three times, in the typical zoo attendee's
Iloveyou! shriek, before noticing your sign:
not llamas but their close relatives, guanacos.
I'm sorry my boyfriend kept calling you
guaca-moles & I'm sorry I found that funny.
I'm sorry, guanacos, for all four of you on display,
your little slice of Syracuse hill looked nothing
like the lush Patagonian plains or grand
Atacama desert lands pictured in your bio.
I'm sorry you were not llama-famous, & stuck
in an underfunded zoo in Upstate New York.
After reading more of your bio, I'm sorry your lives
in the wild weren't so grand either. Your more
hospitable habitats were being destroyed, you
were hunted by fox, puma, mountain lion, & man,
inventive man who used, I'm sorry, your thick
neck skin to make shoes. I'm sorry that
even though it was a stupid-hot day, you
could not demonstrate your most adorable
survival technique—licking the dew
off cacti—as there were no cacti around.
& yet it's true, I watched you, & I'm sorry for
staring as I did, it's just that you somehow
managed to look at once elegant
& weary, I mean each of you sitting so still
with your legs tucked beneath your body,
& then your sleepy eyes. I mean,
the four of you were like a quartet of elderly
duchesses. (I'm sorry, later I looked you up
on the zoo website & found out you were all
males.) I'm sorry, I meant for this to be

an ode, a love letter, & it is, I swear,
but the ways you'd been treated—I knew I
couldn't, on top of all that, lie to you. I didn't
intend to meet you & you yourselves were
probably hoping for better. But isn't this
how it happens? Aren't all great
love stories, at their core,
great mistakes?

Elegy for My Sadness

Maybe the centipede in the cellar
knows with its many disgusting legs
why I am sad. No one else does.
I want to be a sweetheart in every moment,
full of goats & xylophones, as charming
as a hill with a small village on it.
I want to be a village full of sweethearts,
as you are, every second of the day,
cooking me soups & drawing me pictures
& holding me, my inexplicable & elephant sadness,
with your infinite arms.
But isn't it true, you are not
always why I am happy. & I promise
it is true, you are almost never why,
why I am sad. You are just
in the same room with me & my unsweet,
uncharming, completely
uninteresting sadness. I wish it could
unbelong itself from me, unstick
from my face. Who invented the word
"ennui"? A sad Frenchman?
A centipede? They should've never
been born. They should've seen me
in Paris, a sad teenage
exchange student. I was so sad
& so teenaged, one day my host sister
gripped my hand hard & even harder
said, *SOIS HEUREUX.*
BE HAPPY. & miraculously,
I wasn't sad anymore.
All I felt was the desire to slap my host sister.
See, I was angry in Paris, which is clearly
not allowed. One can be sad in Paris (I was)
& one can be in love in Paris (I was not),

but angry? Angry in Paris?
Now, I am in love—with you!—though sometimes
terribly sad for no good reason, & not so much
angry as guilty when you say to me,
Don't cry, don't be sad, as if my sadness
could sink this room, this apartment, this
whole city not Paris. But does my sadness
always need to be your sadness?
I wish I could write an elegy for my sadness
because it has suddenly died. I wish I could mourn it
by kissing you again & again while neither of us
can stop laughing, a kind of kiss where we sometimes
miss the mouth altogether, a kind of kiss
I think every single dead person
in every part of the world must crave
with violent impossibility.

ODE TO MY ENVY

I'm envious of my neighbors who live in a cooler house.
I'm envious of Neruda for having written better poems
& for having lived in a cooler house. I'm envious of poetry

for being more & better than I could ever be. I'm envious
of the redwood who never has to say *I am* & who will
outlive me. I'm envious of those who can consistently resist
pseudo-Buddhist romanticizations of nonhuman entities.

I'm envious of the clouds who can from time to time
fall completely apart & everyone just says, *It's raining*,
& someone might even bring cats & dogs into it,

no one says, *Stop being so dramatic* or *You should see
a professional*. My envy despises your more dramatic
& photogenic envy. My envy desires Olympic gymnast
Danell Leyva's abs. My envy wants to have & be most

Olympic athletes. My envy would be willing to settle
for those who did not make it to the podium. Every day I get
increasingly envious of my friend who dresses so smartly.

Of my friend who's more political. Of my friend who says,
Oh, that's good enough, why am I stressing out? & means it
& stops stressing & is happy. I'm envious of my friend who's
envious of me because he actually wants something I have.

I'm envious of those who learn Life Lessons from their envy.
I'm envious of jealous God & those who always know
the difference between envy & jealousy.

I'm envious of jealous God because although he's been
dead for ages, everyone keeps caring about him, or at least
saying his name, & God knows who'll do that for me,
ten, twenty years after I go.

Irreducible Sociality

No need to remind me of our mutual
friend, the professorial candidate, who's
steeped in the most thoughtful

of French thought, like a plum
in sweet wine, & who thus tells us how
we must bow before the Other or else risk

our own dehumanization. I know.
But must we really go, on this hellishly
cold winter's night, to your coworker's

going-away, in a tiny downtown bar
where all must jostle for a spot, & nothing
good is ever played on the jukebox?

OK, OK. With great humanitarian effort,
I too put on my heavy coat, ready to step
out. But then you kiss me, & we fall, flop,

our altruistic gesture dropped, giving way
to cuddling, again. It seems tonight
that neither of us can embrace more than

one Other, no matter how fine it sounds
in French. So can't we just stay in bed,
in our coats, pressed against each

(singular) Other, & otherwise adhering to
Sartre's *l'enfer c'est les autres*, till we fall asleep
& dream that we went, that our

dream-throats drank down an appropriately
wild amount of beer, & our dream-hands
threw, one stunning fluke round, a winning

dart? & afterwards, we texted everyone:
Don't be a stranger, but be
strange. Come by often for a cup of tea,

in all your unbridled unknowability.

ANTARCTICA

Have the sleepwalking deer returned?
Are those their bluish hoofprints, their crowns

of bone? Has the lost jockey returned? I think
I can hear him, racing between

the lung-shaped trees. Has the cartographer's
grandmother walked back

through those trees? Is the wait
over? Is that a letter from Fernando Pessoa

or the one I need? Has Antarctica returned?
Is that you, Antarctica, trying so hard

to make it back to me? & if so, what will I do?
Will I just have to make room?

Do I have any left? Are all my old shoes
walking back up the back steps of my house?

Did they ever leave or was that only
a sad song I sang once?

Has the Russian driving coach
returned from his long cigarette break?

Has he come back to yell at me for every mistake,
Do you want to be in the life

or in the death?
Has Chen Chen returned? & if not, when

will he? It's time someone told him
the red hat he loved

is no longer his. The lonely weatherman
took it & wears it, most every day.

SECOND THOUGHTS ON A WINTER AFTERNOON

Your mother is sick & all I can think of is how sick's
also a word for "cool," like "ill," though maybe "ill"

is becoming outdated, & "sick" too, & actually it's a lie
I can only think of that, I can also think of my mother,

how your mother's pancreatic cancer doesn't sound
as pretty as the problem my mother has with her heart,

heartbeat, & I can even think my mother has it tougher,
though it isn't cancer, & of course I'd think that, she's mom,

mommy, though of course this woman is mom, mommy
to you, & mommy is very sick, & actually I hate how words

get outdated or we outgrow them, & think you do, too,
saying things like "poochie" & "good gravy," & maybe that's why I

call you sweetie pie & you call me sweet baby, & how can we
make things stay? how can I, when my brain is all wind, drift—

while you're on the phone with thoughtful relatives, I try to
sit, think nothing, but then notice dust swirling in a beam

of bright, so think, as I've thought since mom once told me,
that the light made the dust rise, dance, beautiful—

when on second thought, I can see the dust was just there,
just dirt, & the light only made it visible.

IN THE CITY

for Monica Sok

These bridges are a feat of engineering. These pork & chive dumplings
      we bought together, before hopping on a train
& crossing bridges, are a feat of engineering. Talking to you, crossing bridges
      in trains, eating pork & chive dumplings in your bright boxcar
of a kitchen in Brooklyn, is an engineer's dream-feat
      of astonishment. Tonight I cannot believe
the skyline because the skyline believes in me, forgives me my drooling
      astonishment over it & over the fact that this happens,
this night, every night, its belief, glittering mad & megawatt like the dreams
      of parents. By the way, is this soy sauce
reduced sodium? Do you know? Do we care? High, unabashed sodium intake!
      Unabashed exclamation points! New York is an exclamation
I take, making my escape, away from the quiet snowy commas of Upstate
      & the mess of questions marking my Bostonian past.
In New York we read Darwish, we write broken sonnets finally forgiving
      the Broken English of Our Mothers, we eat
pork & chive dumplings, & I know, it's such a 90s fantasy
      of multiculturalism that I am
rehashing, but still, in New York I feel I can tell you how my mother & I
      used to make dumplings together, like a scene
out of *The Joy Luck Club*. The small kitchen, the small bowl of water
      between us. How we dipped index finger, thumb.
Sealed each dumpling like tucking in a secret, goodnight.
      The meat of a memory. A feat of engineering.
A dream of mother & son. Interrupted by the father, my father
      who made my mother get on a plane, a theory,
years of nowhere across American No's, a degree that proved useless.
      Proved he was the father. I try to build a bridge
to my parents but only reach my mother & it's a bridge she's about to
      jump off of. I run to her, she jumps, she's
swimming, saying, *Finally I've learned—all this time, trying to get from one useless*
      chunk of land to another, when I should've stayed
in the water. & we're drinking tap water in your bright Brooklyn kitchen.
      I don't know what to tell you. I thought I could

tell this story, give it a way out of itself. Even here, in my fabulous
     Tony-winning monologue of a New York, I'm struggling to get
to the Joy, the Luck. I tell you my mother still
     boils the water, though she knows she doesn't have to anymore.
Her special kettle boils in no time, is a feat of engineering.
     She could boil my father in it
& he'd come out a better person, in beautiful shoes.
     She could boil the Atlantic, the Pacific, every idyllic
American pond with its swans. She would.

THE CUCKOO CRY

Lost the milk, spilled my marbles, *our thoughts are fragile*
says the Russian prof, & I try to gather, hold tender
both spilled & lost, my ugly diptych of spring,

every spring my windows open & ugly happens,
I try to hold it together, though maybe should let it go,
gush, let spring bark & heat rain from pit-stained

clouds, let the lark, no, the cuckoo cry.
Let spring say (the truth) I called my mother
a bitch. Said everyone in the neighborhood knew.

She had almost struck down my door, asking who
was on the phone, who, she had struck me,
called me names, forbidden me from talking

(WHO) on the phone, some boy wasn't it,
sick boy spreading his sick musky spring,
American spring, beastly goo of wrong wanting.

Spring says I told my mother she was living in
a dream, could never go back to the way things were.
& she said, *Not even here? I can't say what I feel,*

here, the one place I have in this stupid country,
I can't just be, rest, I have to fight, even at home?
Spring says it doesn't want to be personified,

wants to be forgotten. Doesn't want to be trigger
for memory. Spring says it & fall are retracting
their contractual smells & birds, their unlimited

catalogue of liminal spaces. Fall says, *Stop*
naming children after me. I say, *People name*
their kids Autumn, not Fall.

DIDIER ET ZIZOU

for Zach Horvitz

We loved *Howl* & the Tao when it was still
spelled with a T. We loved green tea but often had
Orangina instead. We loved Trakl & a darkly

declarative sentence. We loved different genders
but knew we were just two variations on the theme,
horny teenage boy. We loved Heidegger

& dwelling in your kitchen, drinking Orangina,
being there, for an hour, two, being moved
by each other's stillnesses.

Sometimes your cat stopped by, ink black
& unimpressed. An ellipsis from next door always
stopped by. It said nothing & preferred to stand,

quietly vibrating, between our adolescent musings
& philosophical urges. Then it reminded us
we had French homework. The future perfect

vs. the plain future. We put off both.
In French one afternoon, when Madame asked for
everyday associations with the season of *l'automne*,

our classmates responded with leaves, scarves, pumpkins,
pumpkin-flavored drinks. Then I raised my hand
& Madame sighed, *Oui, Didier?* & I said, *La mort*, autumn

has to do with death. & you laughed, loud. In French
I was Didier & you were Zizou & Madame was
unimpressed, unamused. In French it was like

we'd never left your kitchen. Except it was raining,
always a panicky autumnal rain with Madame, which
made us crave tea & love e.e. & consider the smallness

of our hands. They were like ellipses, master
procrastinators, unable to finish things & not wanting to,
they loved fooling with the point, multiplying

the period . . . elongating the time . . . the words spent together

KAFKA'S AXE & MICHAEL'S VEST

for Michael Burkard

Still winter. Snowing, still. Can it even be called action, this patience
in the form of gravity overdressed in gray?

Days like this, the right silence can be an action, an axe,
right through the frozen sea, as Kafka calls for. A necessary smashing,
opening. Though silence can also be a shattering, closing.

Think of peace & how the Buddhists say it is found through silence.
Think of silence & how Audre Lorde says it will not protect you.

Think of silence as a violence, when silence means being made
a frozen sea. Think of speaking as a violence, when speaking is a house
that dresses your life in the tidiest wallpaper. It makes your grief

sit down, this house. It makes you chairs when you need
justice. It keeps your rage room temperature. I've been thinking

about how the world is actually unbearable.
About all those moments of silence we're supposed to take.
Each year, more moments, less life, & perhaps

the most monastic of monks are right to take vows
of silence that last a decade.

Though someone else (probably French) says our speaking
was never ours; our thoughts & selves housed
by history, rooms we did not choose, but must live in.

Think of Paul Celan, living
in the bone-rooms of German. Living, singing.

What does it mean, to sing in the language of those
who have killed your mother,
would kill her again? Does meaning shatter, leaving

behind the barest moan? This English, I bear it, a master's
axe, yet so is every tongue—red with singing & killing.

Are we even built for peace? I think of breath & my teacher,
Michael, one of the least masterly, most peaceful people I know,
& Kafka's number one fan. I think of the puffy blue vest Michael wears

when his breaths turn white. Even when I'm doing my best
to think axes & walls, brave monks & unbearable houses,

the thought of Michael in his bit-too-big deep blue vest
leaks in. & I don't think I will ever stop trying to sneak
into casual conversation the word "ululation." If only all language

could be ululation in blue vests. If silence could always be
as quiet as Michael, sitting with his coffee & his book, rereading.

POEM

Racked by doubt, but not yet
wrecked by it, I pray to
the microwave, the crisper
drawer, the lemony
dish soap, please, fish me
out of this funk so I can
stop puttering around the kitchen,
scarfing fries, chips, every
manmade form of potato,
including mashed, even
stuffed, doubled over
by dour, but not yet
doomed to it, I mope with
some hope, desperately open
to the dinkiest sign,
trace of sensation,
confession: I have succumbed
to the starch, I have worn the same
band tee four days in a row,
no one outside the apartment
to see, & here you might
plead, But wait, & beg, But what
about your lover, your recent career luck,
& I'd reply, don't you know
I hate the words "career" & "lover,"
I thought you were my best friend,
but you're just a paperback copy
of *Madame Bovary*
I haven't been able to finish,
I've been putting off
her suicide for weeks now,
it's unbearable to know
how someone will die, even a
made-up someone who does
unlikeable things, it's awful

knowing how & when & a large
portion of why,
& really, "boyfriend" isn't much
better, it sounds like we're still
preparing for junior prom,
when we live together,
& his mother has
no white blood cells because
the chemo that's killing the cancer
is also killing her,
& I should be praying
for her, & sometimes I do,
but mostly it's for me,
the least I could do is not droop
& wilt like a bad houseplant,
it doesn't give people any
strength, this sad
endlessly selfish syntax,
though maybe it's getting
better, I used to think I knew
how I would die,
all tragic like Emma
Bovary, but without all
the adultery in carriages,
& probably not
in provincial France,
& not that I now believe it's
selfish to kill yourself,
I don't know,
don't want to know
how anyone will die or when,
though I'd like to know generally
why, our lives pathetically
brief, compared to the bowhead
whale, the baobab tree,
perhaps "partner" is close
to what I mean, but it sounds so
unsexy, I'd like to sound

sexy again, & strong,
last week when his mother
had a break from chemo,
she went beeline to the grocery,
craving the most un-hospital
of ingredients, hungering
to make some real thing
& hot, but she couldn't touch
anything which could get her
sick, which was potentially
everything, no I don't want
anyone to die, except Cheney
& racist cops & certain
Wall St. bastards &
the guy who called me
a fag, & laughed, but they
will die, & you, & I
don't want to know
how the book ends,
that the book ends, I should pick
up the phone & call my
mother, ask her about
her little vegetable patch
out back, if she's planted
any more eggplants

IN SEARCH OF THE LEAST ABANDONED CONSTELLATION

The rain falls on & off in the western city. The train slips
in & out of tunnels throughout the city. The reader falls endlessly
into her book. The train is an accordion, playing the silence
of adult waiting. The train is a giant ant, wearing an exoskeleton
of polite faces peering out. The reader's face is not among them.

The reader's face is a child's rapt face. The book is her latest
soul, disguised as a more or less acceptable concrete object.
The child is happy. The afternoon, a novel.

The open page rains & creates another, softer city. The child is held
cool & weightless in the arms of the novel, while the parents are
so classic with worry—*How will our child be a doctor &/or lawyer now?*
Support us when we are old? The parents watch people run,
rushing to catch the train. The people's faces deer-like with panic,

relief. The child reads & reads, does not understand completely.
She has no need. The parents wish for stillness, then movement
for their child, then themselves. They peer over their child's shoulder

& catch the words, *They were in search of the least abandoned constellation.*
The parents wait for the child to become a western bird, but the child
keeps leaking into a northern lake. In the novel, a central adult is writing
a strange letter because her parents have died. A deeply impossible thing
to the child reading, but she manages to suspend her disbelief.

The adult in the novel reads over her letter, unsure of the words—
Now that you are not even the rain, what train can I take? Remember
when we were morning after morning of such ordinary waiting,

of hair still wet in the April light & suitcases held tight?

music of the word "callipygian,"
which means the having of well-shaped buttocks.
I will miss the particular cruelty

of tongue twisters in my first tongue:
"Shíshì shīshì Shī Shì, shì shī, shì shí shí shī.
Shì shíshí shì shì shì shī."

I will miss the particularly high volume
YES of correctly completing this tongue twister,
even once. & the deadpan ditty

of the English translation: "Mr. Shi, the poet
from a stone den, likes to eat lions. He pledges
solemnly to eat ten lions. Regularly

he goes to the market to look at the lions."
I will miss the roar of those lions,
hungering for freedom

while Mr. Shi hungers for them. & outside
the market, on a nearby street, the bright
ding-ding of a bicycle bell. & the messenger

singing, *A telegram, a telegram
from overseas . . .*
& the sound of the sea.

The sound the sea makes at night,
delivering its own telegrams—
a sort of sensual

moo. I will miss the particular quiet
of my body, your body, opening
a window to listen.

FROG-HOPPING GRAVESTONES

after Bert Hardy

The schoolboys in the cemetery look happily busy, playing what looks like the last game of tag on earth—one in which the rules are reversed & almost all of them get to be It. The photographer has caught them rushing between the gravestones, a swarm of prim haircuts, tailored pants, & recently polished shoes now getting sullied. This uniformed, many-armed It chases while one lone boy has scurried up a tree, his arms & knees hugging tight the bark, the darkest part of the picture.

Or maybe this is the wrong song, the tree-climbing & graveyard-running unrelated, the schoolboys forming separate scenes. For what to make of the boy, a bit older perhaps, who's just standing, staring at a gravestone? Does he recognize the name? For what to make of the boy frog-hopping a gravestone? He's the sole hopper, & yet it's his action that gives the photograph its name, gives this playground at the end of the world its loudest life: one boy pushing off the top of a gravestone with both hands, one boy's legs kicking out, one boy flying, flinging himself in an impossible direction, a future outside the photograph—

SORROW SONG WITH OPTIMUS PRIME

You are an unhappy thing, cursed with legs,
every step carrying the love who left, the love you left,
the job lost, the mountain of low, the mounting lack.
But your legs grow tired of holding it, so you transfer it
to your head. Then your head grows tired, so you delegate it
to your shoulders. Then they are tired & you are tired
& you don't know what to do but replant it in your legs,
your feet, & walk it to the supermarket.
You try to sell your sickness to the octopus
whose tentacles lie in severed strips. But he refuses.
You try to freeze your darkness but the industrial fridge
spits it out. You put a pink hat on your gloom
& march it to the toy store where you try giving it away,
giving it back to the latest version of the unattainable
robot from childhood, the truck that transforms, grows
arms that hold laser guns, could hold your grief, you.
But the sorrow is held by your heart now, your own
exquisite machine that seems finally to contain it.
Then even your most stubborn muscle grows weary, & sends it
whirling through your bloodstream & your blood carries it,
everywhere in your body at once, so there is no more moving.
So you sit, on the floor of the toy store, like the end
of an avalanche, each rock, tree, & small wish of you
crushed, heaped. & the scream of your total defeat
is the cry that brought the mountain down.

3

FOR I WILL DO/UNDO WHAT WAS DONE/UNDONE TO ME

i pledge allegiance to the already fallen snow
& to the snow now falling. to the old snow & the new.
to foot & paw & tire prints in the snow both young & aging,
the deep & shallow marks left on cold streets, our long

misbegotten manuscripts. i pledge allegiance to the weather
report that promises more snow, plus freezing rain.
though i would minus the pluvial & plus the multitude

of messages pressed muddy into the perfectly
mutable snow, i have faith in the report that goes on to read:
by the end of the week, there will be an increased storm-related
illegibility of the asphalt & concrete & brick. for i pledge

betrayal to the fantasy of ever reading anything
completely. for i will do/undo what was done/undone to me:
to be brought into a patterned world of weathers

& reports. & thus i pledge allegiance to the always
partial, the always translated, the always never
of knowing who's walking around, what's being left behind,
the signs, the cries, the breadcrumbs & the blood. the toe-

nails & armpit hair of our trying & failing to speak
our specks of *here* to the *everywhere*. dirty snow of my weary
city, i ask you to tell me a story about your life

& you tell me you've left for another country,
but forgot your suitcase. at the airport they told you
not to worry, all your things have already been sent
to your new place by your ninth-grade french teacher,

the only nice one. & the weather where your true love is
is governed by principles or persons you can't name,

imagine. it is that good, or bad.

People person seeks paid internship in liking you as a friend,
     respecting you as a coworker. Serial monogamist
seeks change of pace in slutting it up for the summer.
     Animal lover seeks entry-level position, teaching guinea pigs
how to swim. Solitude lover seeks more of the same.
     I want to be as beautiful as carrot cake. As three firefighters
shoveling out a fire hydrant after the snowstorm.
     As the whole city after storm.
I am knowledgeable in advanced aftermath. I am proficient
     in scowling. Often I am a counterculture pistachio
on casual Friday. In one pocket, chapstick. In the other, racist comments
     from people who claim to be postracial. Or kind.
If you'd like I can alphabetize all my regrets but I'll have to start from *H*.
     I like a good multipurpose room. Also multipurpose flour.
I excel at pouring tea into the moon. A scary amount. I am too much
     statuary in not enough city. I am a collection of collectors.
It's pretty okay. One of my collectors is collecting rust from radiators.
     & belief from Quakers. I've befriended every shade of evening
& they cannot recommend me highly enough. I hold degrees in
     both my hands. In my mouth. My sole weakness is being
the chairperson of my own childhood. Beloved president of ages 3
     through 7. My weakness is hoarding phrases I've
overheard / didn't want to read. *Now! even softer & more absorbent!*
     Our finest, the supermarket brand says, like from one family
to another. I am a family of collectors. My father collects
     newspapers. Like they're his own memories. We trip
over stacks of them in the living room. Groan
     when he quotes from them, all housing markets & cloud formations.
Car prices are a specialty he whips out for dinner guests.
     My weakness is that I listen.
My mother collects, no, saves stamps. Like they're her own
     children. But better: she can store them in a book, take them out when
she wants. Love them like they've just been born. & the labor,
     a breeze: no drugs, no doctor, just a pair of scissors, a bucket,

warm water. All the wonderment of birth in under 20 minutes.

    The mother doesn't even have to be physically present. She can go check
on her human kids while the water coaxes, releases

    the stamps from the remaining blocks of envelope. She returns
& the bucket is a small aquarium of state birds & flowers,

    dead presidents & once popular singers.
My weakness is anything paper & anything miniature.

    My parents' friend's weakness is nautical paintings & antique clocks.
My boyfriend's stepfather's weakness is vintage farm equipment

    & antique clocks. I want them to meet. Perhaps I could be
a liaison. Or something else French. In this economy

    of acute magpie syndrome. Where "just a hobby" is the strongest
industry. & we work overtime at our reverie.

    My weakness is loving this economy.
I want them to meet but I only see my parents' friend

    at Thanksgiving. We'll be in the middle of turkey & mapo tofu
when all the old weird clocks go off. No, not all.

    Some go off on time at 6:00. Others at 6:01. & the last, rebellious group,
6:03. At first I think this is a deliberate unsynchronized

    idiosyncrasy. But at the next Thanksgiving, when this occurs
again, our host exclaims in his most

    New England Mandarin, *Oh dear. I thought
I'd fixed them. Sorry about that. Our clocks,* he sighs,

    as though they belong to everyone at the table, everyone.

from your grandmother's coat. You worry with your thumb the stranger's page. Aging spine of the black sky, night-burps of the sleeping computer. Don't listen to the judgment of your scraped knees. Night anchors in your belly button, your pubic hair. Stars snore safely, for years. Your smile in the early dark is a paraphrase of Mars. Your smile in the deep dark is an anagram of Jupiter. My worst simile is that I'm fancy like a piece of salami wearing a tuxedo. Waiting with a cone of gelato. Your smile in the dreaming dark is an umbrella for all the going, gone, & yet to come. Orioles come for the oranges you've placed in the arms of the architect. Which birds will you pull into orbit tomorrow? You try to sew the night onto your own coat, but it won't stay. Too much memory weather, werewolf migration. You itch for the window's shore. You row, the growing light rearranging your voice, the rain your lunatic photographer.

THINGS STUCK IN OTHER THINGS WHERE THEY DON'T BELONG

My mother one afternoon in a cowboy hat, sitting on a Texan bench of hay.
Me in the same configuration of time, space, & cowboy hat.
The memory in my brain like a boulder in a haystack, like a bad joke.
The sun in our faces.
The year we spent in Fort Worth, Texas, our first year in Měiguó.
The fluent Not-English I spoke in kindergarten.
The blond boy from Germany in the same sandbox with me, laughing at my jokes.
His name, Eammon, like *Amen*, unlike any Chinese or American name
I'd ever heard, a ticklish raindrop
in my ears.
The soy sauce + Tabasco sauce + mud in my "soups."
The same ingredients + sugar in my "pies."
Me in the biggest kitchen I'd ever seen, running around the "island,"
chased by an elderly white man my father said to call my "Texas grandpa."
My father with his full head of black hair & British-inflected English
in the graduate religion program at Texas Christian University.
The grease-tang of kung pao chicken in my mother's shirts,
in my mother's far-away look, after shifts.
The Bengal tigers in the tightly fenced "forest habitat" in the zoo Eammon & I
      visited.
The sand in our shoes, the sun in our faces
as we sweated over castle fortification, all afternoon.
The *Goodbye* I placed in Eammon's ear.
The motels & motels I played Power Rangers in, leaving Texas
because my father had won a scholarship.
The way I came to learn the French word for "scar"
by seeing it over & over in a French *Harry Potter*, in my American head,
in the small bald spot on the left side of my head,
which I received one afternoon in Texas,
when I was the skinniest, sincerest Superman, & flew into the kitchen
where my mother was removing from the stove
a saucepan of milk, still boiling,
& we bumped into each other—"cicatrice."
The cicatrice of Eammon's Christmas card, once kept bedside,

now in a box, a basement.
My dream in the motels that my father's scholarship
was a type of ship & soon we'd get to ride it
& reach Massachusetts, a vast
snowy island.

SONG OF THE NIGHT'S GIFT

The blind dog, the black ink, the boldly
silly sort of hope I had as a child,
as on a holiday, so greedily spent

I forgot to fear abandonment
& abandoned myself beautifully
to sleep, to black night gleaming

with my father's eyes, his hands
& strange labor, an alchemy of stone
to river, then his quick brush, the black

words, I dreamt greedily, I still dream
of it, though it's been years since I've
seen it, & perhaps, it never happened,

was simply & always, a blind gift
of the black night, a "memory"
I cherish like a pet, a small guardian

to help banish the day, the fear
that my father will be abandoned
& no alchemy will reach.

Chapter VIII

Autumn was an argument about hair & how much of it.
Too much not enough just right but just for now & then it was winter.
The licorice of every season was rather inappropriate.
Well OK how about this. & you put on more of my deodorant.
What can one do but put on more deodorant?
Paris, lopsided, was still Paris. A congregation, a conflagration.
A smiling conundrum in the form of a ladder it takes years
to climb down. In our last (ever) Scrabble game, you changed my "whore"
into "whored." I tried to ask my parents to leave the room,
but not my life. It was very hard. Because the room was the size
of my life. Because my life was small. & wanted to eat candy corn
instead of confrontation. Raising one's voice in a small space
felt at once godlike & childish. You agreed with me
out of a practical concern. & I loved you for it. We were two
horses in search of the least abandoned constellation.
But the night sky was overtaken by the beatitude of the ultimate horse.
Also Ben had upset Wes with his choice of neckties but then
the author decided it would all be better in second person actually.
When did I first realize my parents were not infinite?
That I could see the end of them? Past their capes & catchphrases?
One day in fourth grade my teacher said, *You're lucky to be*
so young. You'll heal up from that bicycle accident in no time. No scars.
No time. No scars. Sing it with me. Loud as Reykjavík summer.
Easy as my Etch A Sketch when I made a mistake.
I will try my best not to mistake you for my parents I mean my problems
with my parents I mean me. Believe with me another
melody. That the room, the life could go by a different light
& we could say *hello*. Meaning *gentleness* with all our might.

NATURE POEM

The birds insist on pecking the wooded dark. The wooded dark
pecks back. *It is time to show the universe what you are capable of,*
says my horoscope, increasingly insistent this month.
But what I am capable of is staring

at the salt accident on the coffee table & thinking,
What sad salt. I admire my horoscope
for its conviction. I envy its consistency. Every day. Every day,
there is a future to be aggressively vaguer about.

Earlier today, outside the cabin, the sudden deer were a supreme
headache of beauty. Don't they know I am trying to be alone
& at peace? In theory I am alone & really I am hidden,
which is a fine temporary substitute for peace, except I still

have email, which is how I receive my horoscope, & even here
in the wooded dark I receive yet another email mistaking me
for another Chen. I add this to a folder, which also includes
emails sent to my address but addressed to Chang,

Chin, Cheung. Once, in a Starbucks, the cashier
was convinced I was Chad. Once, in a Starbucks, the cashier
did not quite finish the n on my Chen, & when my tall mocha was ready,
they called out for Cher. I preferred this by far, but began to think

the problem was Starbucks. Why can't you see me? Why can't I stop
needing you to see me? For someone who looks like you
to look at me, even as the coffee accident
is happening to my second favorite shirt?

In my wooded dark, I try insisting on a supremely tall,
never-lonely someone. But every kind of someone needs
someone else to insist with. I need. If not the you
I have memorized & recited & mistaken

for the universe—another you.

When I Grow Up I Want to Be a List of Further Possibilities

To be a good
ex/current friend for R. To be one last

inspired way to get back at R. To be relationship
advice for L. To be advice

for my mother. To be a more comfortable
hospital bed for my mother. To be

no more hospital beds. To be, in my spare time,
America for my uncle, who wants to be China

for me. To be a country of trafficless roads
& a sports car for my aunt, who likes to go

fast. To be a cyclone
of laughter when my parents say

their new coworker is *like that*, they can tell
because he wears pink socks, see, you don't, so you can't,

can't be one of them. To be the one
my parents raised me to be—

a season from the planet
of planet-sized storms.

To be a backpack of PB&J & every
thing I know, for my brothers, who are becoming

their own storms. To be, for me, nobody,
homebody, body in bed watching TV. To go 2D

& be a painting, an amateur's hilltop & stars,
simple decoration for the new apartment

with you. To be close, J.,
to everything that is close to you—

blue blanket, red cup, green shoes
with pink laces.

To be the blue & the red.
The green, the hot pink.

FOR I WILL CONSIDER MY BOYFRIEND JEFFREY

after Christopher Smart's Jubilate Agno, Fragment B,
[For I will consider my Cat Jeoffry]

For I will consider my boyfriend Jeffrey.

For he is an atheist but makes room for the unseen, unsayable.

For he is a vegetarian but makes room for half-off Mondays at the conveyor belt sushi place.

For he must vacuum/mop/scrub/rinse/hand sanitize/air freshen the entire apartment to deal with the stress of having received a traffic ticket.

For he dances in his seat while driving us to the supermarket.

For he despises tarantulas, sharks, flying on planes, & flightless birds such as the cassowary of New Guinea, which he has only seen in videos & thinks looks like "a goddamn velociraptor."

For he likes to claim he is the butch one.

For he is Jeffrey Gilbert of Gilbertsville, New York.

For he lets his beard grow.

For when his beard has grown up & down & out, he takes a tenderly long time to shave.

For this he performs in ten steps.

For first he looks upon his furry countenance to assess & accept the difficult journey that lies before him.

For secondly he washes with holistic care his whole foxy face.

For thirdly he applies as much shaving cream as I use in a month.

For fourthly he puts on Erik Satie or LCD Soundsystem.

For fifthly he sways a little, to the music, before lifting to his cheek the buzzing razor.

For sixthly he shaves.

For seventhly he shaves.

For eighthly he shaves.

For ninthly he shaves, then asks me to come help.

For tenthly he holds back a giggle while I tickle the back of his neck with the buzzing razor.

For having shaved, he declares that he is ready to get back to work.

For his work involves many instruments, including a large, completely unnecessary keytar, or keyboard guitar, which he plays beautifully.

For he plays & then transfers his playing onto a computer, where he works on it further.

For he wears big headphones like little moons on his ears & begins to bounce
in his chair for the room is becoming a continent of rhythms & almost-
meanings & just-discovered birds only he can hear.
For though he does not fare well on planes he will fly to those he loves.
For his beard is already growing back.
For he looks happy & doesn't know I'm looking & that makes his happiness free.

BABEL & JUICE

undo me
left & sight
north & mouth
uncompass me
with your tender
your further
& sideways
impossibilities
come on
murk me blue me
knock me out out
of me my
tight &
goodly just sweetly
behead me
with your babel
& juice your fiddle
your ruse your
arson your trees your
armpits your fishes
your loco your lilts
your mango
your licks

Song of the Anti-Sisyphus

I want to start a snowball fight with you, late at night
in the supermarket parking lot. I want you
to do your worst. I want to put the groceries in the car first

because it's going to get nasty. Because I was reading today
in the science section of the paper that passionate love
lasts only a year, maybe two, if you're lucky.

Because I want to be extra, extra lucky. Because the article
apologized specifically to poets—sorry, you hopeless
saps—as though we automatically believe in love more

than anyone else (more than kindergarten teachers, long-haired
carpenters) & have been pushing this Non-Truth
on everyone. Because who knows what will happen,

but I want to, baby, want to believe it's always possible
to love bigger & madder, even after two, three, four years,
four decades. I want a love as dirty as a snowball fight

in the sludge, under grimy yellow lights. I want this winter
inside my lungs. Inside my brain & dream. I want to eat
the unplowed street & the fog that's been erasing

evergreens. I want to eat the fog only to discover
it's some giant's lost silver blanket. I want to
find the giant & return to him his treasure.

I want the journey to be long. & strange, like a map
drawn in snow by our shadows shivering. I want to shiver
against you, into you. I want the sound

of your teeth. I want the sound of the wind. I want to be
like the kids with their plastic sleds, gliding down,
all the way down the hill, then trudging

their sleds & snowsuited bodies all the way
back to the top. I want to be how they do this, for hours,
till sunset, till some sensible someone has

to come drag them away from the snow, the slope,
the 3 . . .   2 . . .   1!
of joy. I want to be the Anti-Sisyphus, in love

with repetition, in love, in love. Foolish repetition,
wise repetition. I want more hours, I want insomnia, I want
to replace the clock tick with tambourines. I want to growl,

moan, whisper, grunt, hum, & howl your name.
I want again & again your little dance, little booty shake
in big snow boots, as I sing your name.

TALKING TO GOD ABOUT HEAVEN FROM THE BED OF A HEATHEN

You should know that although I miraculously
agreed to attend Bible camp one summer (my devoutly

pragmatic parents signed me up because the camp was free),
I don't & have never believed in you. Yet here I am:

sitting up in bed, thinking about death, & needing
to talk to someone who (reportedly) has the inside story.

I know, though, that there are believers who don't believe
out of fear solely. They actually love you. They reach out

& receive your touch. Like a friend, like a boyfriend, like the boy
beside me, overheating, reeking of sweat, & still (somehow)

asleep. I wish I could feel your warmth, as easily
as I feel his. But I don't. I feel fear. I hear fear telling me I'm

a body, that's all. & the boy I love is a body. & bodies die. No
other world, no return to this world in another form. (Annihilation.)

It isn't that I didn't think these were the facts before. It's that now,
he's here. I have to try harder. Believe the facts could be

at least a little wrong. Please, something. Some
magic, real as this ripe life with him.

Elegy to Be Exhaled at Dusk

I am an elegy to be exhaled at dusk. I am an elegy to be written on a late
October leaf. An elegy to be blown

from its tree by a late October wind. To be stomped on & through
by passersby old & young

& dead & unborn. To be crinkled & crushed into tiny brown-
orange pieces. & then

collected, painstakingly, no, pain*fully*, piece by piece, & assembled like
a puzzle or collage or

Egyptian god, but always incomplete, always a few bits & limbs
missing. An elegy to be

misplaced, stuffed away in the attic's memory, & only brought out again
once every occupant of the house has

ceased. Yes, I am an elegy properly architectured by ruin. An elegy that has
experienced crows & lake effect

snow, an elegy that has seen Ukrainian snow falling on the forehead
of Paul Celan, Paul Celan's mother,

the German tongue, the tangled tongues of all your literary
& literal ancestors—but more

than that, an elegy that has felt light, the early morning light falling
on your lovely someone's

lovable bare feet as he walks across the wood floor to sit by the window,
by the plants, with a cup of jasmine

& a book he will barely open but love to hold the weight of
in his lap. I am,

my friend, an elegy that has taken into account, into heart & October wind,
the weight of someone's soft

hair-covered head in someone else's warm, welcoming lap.

Spell to Find Family

for Kundiman

I thirst for the starlight
that opens elephant skin.
I thirst for the raven

conjugated into riven
by summer storm.
My job is to trick adults

into knowing they have
hearts. My heart whose
irregular plural form is

Hermes. My Hermes
whose mouths are wings
& thieves, begging

the moon for a flood
of wolves, the reddest
honey. My job is to trick

myself into believing
there are new ways
to find impossible honey.

For I do not know all the faces
of my family, on this earth.
Perhaps it will take a lifetime

(or five) to discover every
sister, brother. Heartbeat
elephantine, serpentine,

opposite of saturnine.
I drive in the downpour,
the road conjugated

into uproar, by hearts
I do not know.
By the guttural & gargantuan

highway lion. The 18-wheeler
whose shawl of mist is a mane
of newborn grandmothers.

LITTLE SONG

I am sitting in the grass   I hear a microwave from the house   Someone setting the time
Then changing their mind   Little song of beeps   The bees come to visit the hydrangeas
They're a loopy lopsided equation   that actually works out   that is the foundation
of the universe   The bees decide to visit me   I try to stay still so they can visit properly
& am returned to my body   the squishy cantaloupe depths   the memory of when I was a kid
the days of excitement over the phrase "centrifugal force"   I think it was my #1 phrase
for a week   I started telling people that was where babies came from   My father the scholar
shook his head   & explained capital N- Nature   yin & yang   *You must have opposites* he said
For years I thought gay people didn't exist in China   But then I went to a nightclub
in Shanghai   small   & literally underground   but packed   with gorgeous men   Chinese men
a winding techno garden of them   Only women my straight friend   & the hardworking old lady
at coat check   I danced till I got sweaty   then too sweaty   In the rest area a man passed by
& pinched my nipple   through my now see-through shirt   I saw how China could be
& Nature could   & me   singing in the grass   little songs about gravity

POEM IN NOISY MOUTHFULS

Can't stop eating you, movie-style extra butter microwave popcorn.
Can't stop watching you, rented movie about an immigrant family
from Lebanon. Can't help but weep, seeing the family wave

goodbye to relatives in the Beirut airport—tear salt mixing with
popcorn salt. Can't hide my mess, myself from the friend beside me.
Can't answer his question, *Does it remind you of your family, leaving China?*

I want to say, *No, it's completely different,* which in many ways it is, but really
I'm remembering what a writer friend once said to me, *All you write about
is being gay or Chinese*—how I can't get over that, & wonder if it's true,

if everything I write is in some way an immigrant narrative or another
coming out story. I recall a recent poem, featuring fishmongers in Seattle,
& that makes me happy—clearly that one isn't about being gay or Chinese.

But then I remember a significant number of Chinese immigrants
live in Seattle & how I found several of the Pike Place fishmongers
attractive when I visited, so I guess that poem's about being gay

& Chinese, too. So I say to my friend, *I'm not sure,* & keep eating
the popcorn. Thank god we chose the giant "family size" bag. Can't stop
the greasy handfuls, noisy mouthfuls. Can't eat popcorn quietly.

Later, during my friend's smoke break, still can't come up with a worthy
response to his radical queer critique of homonormativity, of monogamy,
domesticity, front lawn glory. *These middle-class gays picking out*

garden gnomes, ignoring all the anti-racist work of decolonization
that still needs to be done—don't you think they're lame? I say, *Yeah, for sure,*
but think, marriage, house, 1 kid, 2 cats—how long have I wanted that?

Could I give that up in the name of being a *real* queer? Probably can't.
& it's like another bad habit I can't give up. Eating junk, can't. Procrastinating,
can't. Picking scabs, can't. Being friends with people who challenge

my beliefs & life plans, can't. Reading & believing in Ayn Rand, though?
Can. Brief phase as a Christian because I liked the cross as an accessory? Can.
WWJD? Can. White heterosexist patriarchy? Can. America . . . can't.

Can't help but think, when we get back to the movie, how it was my father's
decision to move here, not my mother's, just like the parents on screen.
Can't stop replaying my mother's walk onto the plane, carrying me,

though I was getting too old for it, holding me, my face pressed into her
hair, her neck, as she cried, quietly—can't stop returning to this scene of leaving,
can't stop pausing the scene, thinking I've left something out again,

something else my mother told me. Like my grandmother at the airport,
how she saw my small body so tied to my mother's body, & still she doubted,
she had to say, *You better not lose him.* & my mother kept that promise

till she couldn't, she lost me, in the new country, but doesn't
that happen to all parents & their children, one way or another,
& don't we need to get lost? Lost, dizzy, stubbly, warm, stumbling,

whoa—that's what it felt like, 17, kissing a boy for the first time.
Can't forget it. Can't forget when my mother found out & said,
This would never have happened if we hadn't come to this country.

But it would've happened, every bit as dizzy, lost, back in China.
It didn't happen because of America, dirty Americans. It was me,
my need. My father said, *You have to change,* but I couldn't, can't

give you up, boys & heat, scruff & sweet. Can't get over you. Trying to get
over what my writer friend said, *All you write about is being gay or Chinese.*
Wish I had thought to say to him, *All you write about is being white*

or an asshole. Wish I had said, *No, I already write about everything—*
& everything is salt, noise, struggle, hair,
carrying, kisses, leaving, myth, popcorn,

mothers, bad habits, questions.

POPLAR STREET

Oh. Sorry. Hello. Are you on your way to work, too?
I was just taken aback by how you also have a briefcase,

also small & brown. I was taken by how you seem, secretly,
to love everything. Are you my new coworker? Oh. I see. No.

Still, good to meet you. I'm trying out this thing where it's good
to meet people. Maybe, beyond briefcases, we have some things

in common. I like jelly beans. I'm afraid of death. I'm afraid
of farting, even around people I love. Do you think your mother

loves you when you fart? Does your mother love you
all the time? Have you ever doubted?

I like that the street we're on is named after a tree,
when there are none, poplar or otherwise. I wonder if a tree

has ever been named after a street, whether that worked out.
If I were a street, I hope I'd get a good name, not Main

or Pleasant. One night I ran out of an apartment,
down North Pleasant Street—it was soft & neighborly

with pines & oaks, it felt too hopeful,
after what happened. After I told my mother I liked a boy

& she said No. You're sick. Get out
before you get your brothers sick. Sometimes, parents & children

become the most common strangers. Eventually,
a street appears where they can meet again.

Or not. Do I love my mother? Do I have to
forgive in order to love? Or do I have to love

for forgiveness to even be possible? What do you think?
I'm trying out this thing where questions about love & forgiveness

are a form of work I'd rather not do alone. I'm trying to say,
Let's put our briefcases on our heads, in the sudden rain,

& continue meeting as if we've just been given our names.

Notes

"Summer Was Forever" (p. 19): The phrase "croissant factory" is borrowed from Frank O'Hara's poem "Lines for the Fortune Cookies."

"If I should die tomorrow, please note that I will miss the particular" (p. 56): The lines *"A telegram, a telegram / from overseas . . ."* are borrowed from W. H. Auden's libretto for Benjamin Britten's operetta *Paul Bunyan.*

◉

Acknowledgments

Many thanks to the editors of the following publications, where poems in this book (often as earlier versions) first appeared:

The Adroit Journal: "Nature Poem," "Song of the Night's Gift";

Bat City Review: "Frog-Hopping Gravestones";

Bear Review: "In the Hospital";

The Best American Poetry 2015: "for i will do/undo what was done/undone to me" (first published in *PANK*);

Breakwater Review: "Elegy for My Sadness," "Song of the Anti-Sisyphus";

Codex Journal: "Irreducible Sociality";

Construction Magazine: "Sorrow Song with Optimus Prime";

Crab Orchard Review: "In Search of the Least Abandoned Constellation";

Cutthroat: A Journal of the Arts: "First Light";

DIAGRAM: "Please take off your shoes before entering   do not disturb";

Drunken Boat: "How I Became Sagacious," "In This Economy";

Dusie: "Little Song";

Fjords Review: "When I Grow Up I Want to Be a List of Further Possibilities";

Fogged Clarity: "Elegy," "West of Schenectady";

Gulf Coast: "Self-Portrait as So Much Potential";

Indiana Review: "In the City," "Poem";

jmww: "Didier et Zizou," "Talking to God About Heaven from the Bed of a Heathen";

The Margins: "Chapter VIII";

The Massachusetts Review: "Second Thoughts on a Winter Afternoon";

Narrative: "Self-Portrait With & Without";

Narrative Northeast: "Kafka's Axe & Michael's Vest," "Things Stuck in Other Things Where They Don't Belong";

Nepantla: A Journal Dedicated to Queer Poets of Color: "Spell to Find Family";

New Delta Review: "Antarctica";

Ostrich Review: "Night falls like a button" (as "Sleeping in the Last of Summer"), "Race to the Tree";

PANK: "babel & juice" (as "poem,/love,"), "Summer Was Forever," "Talented Human Beings" (as "Jerking Off to Koh Masaki");

The Pinch: "Elegy to Be Exhaled at Dusk";

Poetry: "I'm not a religious person but," "Poplar Street";

Print-Oriented Bastards: "Poem in Noisy Mouthfuls";

The Screaming Sheep: "Ode to My Envy";
Southern Indiana Review: "The Cuckoo Cry";
Tupelo Quarterly: "Song with a Lyric from Allen Ginsberg";
Twelfth House: "If I should die tomorrow, please note that I will miss the particular" (as "If I Should Die Tomorrow, Please Know That These Are the Sounds I Will Miss Most From This Good & Outrageous Earth"), "To the Guanacos at the Syracuse Zoo."

"I'm not a religious person but" also appears in *The Poetry Review* (UK), a special issue featuring work first published in *Poetry*. "First Light," "Kafka's Axe & Michael's Vest," "Poplar Street" also appear in *Political Punch: Contemporary Poems on the Politics of Identity*, an anthology published by Sundress Publications in 2016. "Antarctica," "babel & juice," "for i will do/undo what was done/undone to me," "Little Song," "Please take off your shoes before entering   do not disturb," "Sorrow Song with Optimus Prime" also appear in *Kissing the Sphinx*, a chapbook published by Two of Cups Press in 2016. "Race to the Tree," "Spell to Find Family," "Summer Was Forever" also appear in *Set the Garden on Fire*, a chapbook published by Porkbelly Press in 2015.

I am grateful to Nicci Mechler and Leigh Anne Hornfeldt, my incredibly hardworking chapbook editors and publishers, for first believing that my poems have something to say, as bodies of work. I am grateful to Kundiman, Lambda Literary, Tent: Creative Writing, and the Saltonstall Arts Colony for gifts of time and community. I am immensely lucky to have worked with these brilliant teachers: Polina Barskova, Curtis Bauer, Michael Burkard, Kimberly Chang, Floyd Cheung, Katie Cortese, Martín Espada, Aracelis Girmay, Deborah Gorlin, Sarah C. Harwell, Brooks Haxton, Christopher Kennedy, Jacqueline Kolosov, Heather Madden, David Tomas Martinez, Leslie Jill Patterson, Minnie Bruce Pratt, Rachel Rubinstein, George Saunders, Yuan Shu, William Wenthe. Special thanks to Bruce Smith for reading these poems again and again, in the smartest ways. Thanks to class- and workshopmates: Tessa Brown, Grady Chambers, Cassandra de Alba, Nancy Dinan, Patrick Dundon, David Gustavsen, Sophia Holtz, Mark Keats, Carolyn Li-Madeo, Jessica Poli, Yanira Rodriguez, Kate Simonian, Sarah Viren. To all my teachers and fellow writers at Hampshire, Syracuse, and Texas Tech: thank you. To my amazing students: thank you. I would also like to express gratitude to Sherman Alexie for selecting a poem of mine for *The Best American Poetry 2015*; I am also deeply, fiercely grateful for the work by fellow Asian American poets in this anthology—Rajiv Mohabir, Aimee Nezhukumatathil, Monica Youn, Jane

Wong. And I'd like to take the time to acknowledge here the real and brilliant Asian American poet who could have appeared in the anthology instead of the appropriating and exoticizing white American poet who did appear. Crucial, for literature and for living: to think historically, to dream critically, to build more spaces in which more voices are present, more presences dreaming and disturbing what is "known." Many thanks to the people who have asked me to come read, talk, participate, build: Kaveh Akbar, Cynthia Arrieu-King, Cam Awkward-Rich, Erika Jo Brown, Marci Calabretta Cancio-Bello, Doug Paul Case, Julia Kolchinsky Dasbach, Danielle DeTiberus, Duy Doan, David Eye, Mckendy Fils-Aimé, Danielle Legros Georges, Roy Guzmán, Luther Hughes, Peter LaBerge, Iris A. Law, Laurin Macios and others at Mass Poetry, Rachel McKibbens, Erin J. Mullikin, Hieu Minh Nguyen, Sam Sax, Kate Schapira, Danez Smith, Erin Elizabeth Smith and Fox Frazier-Foley, Christopher Soto, Jeremy Tow.

My thanks and my love: Eric Berlin, Gabrielle Friedman, Mag Gabbert, Rupert Giles, Becca Glaser, Zach Horvitz, Anna Jekel, Swati Khurana, Muriel Leung, Trevor Pace, Monica Sok, Caitlin Vance. For entertaining all my wackiness and coming over for brunch and listening to me ramble on about this manuscript, my thanks and my love to Jessica Smith and Sam Herschel Wein. My love and my thanks and my love to Jeff Gilbert. Love, in all the true difficult lucky ways, to my parents and my brothers; to my family, chosen and across oceans.

To Peter Conners, Jenna Fisher, Richard Foerster, Sandy Knight, and everyone at BOA: you've made the dream I had since I was in second grade come true. Endless thanks to Jericho Brown for saying this book should exist and for encouraging me to make the book I want to read.

◙

Milton Keynes UK
Ingram Content Group UK Ltd.
UKHW050335111124
450920UK00001B/1

9 781780 374864